THE *Skin* & THE *Skeleton*

WHAT TO DO WHEN THE LAID-BACK MARRIES THE UP-SET

D1737948

Ken Peters

The Skin & the Skeleton
© 2007 by Ken Peters

Published by Open Heart Ministries
15648 Bombay Blvd.
S. Beloit, IL 61080
www.ohmint.org
benrpeters@juno.com

All rights reserved. No part of this publication may be reproduced
or transmitted in any form or by any means without permission of
the publisher.

ISBN: 978-0-9789884-1-8

Unless otherwise indicated, Bible quotations are taken from the
New King James Version. Copyright © 1983 by Thomas Nelson, Inc.

Contents

Section 3 ~ Prevention

Acknowledgments

There are many people I would like to thank for helping me with this book. I thank my wife, Valencia, who is beautiful inside and out. During the past 13 years of marriage, she has been with me every step of the way and together we have discovered Biblical insights and Kingdom principles that nurture Godly marriages. I thank my parents, Ben & Brenda Peters, for raising me up in the House of God and for modeling a lasting marriage. I thank my spiritual father, Pastor Mike Hayes from Covenant Church Carrollton, TX, for teaching me the Word of God. His ministry has literally changed my life, and I am and will continue to be a true son in the faith. I thank Gordon Emerson for all the long hours spent on editing this book. And I thank the wonderful folks of Covenant Church Spokane for allowing me to serve you each week as together we explore and apply Kingdom principles to our lives.

Introduction

This Book is for Extreme Opposites!

Did you marry someone who seems to be the complete opposite of you? Is one of you a laid-back person while the other is a bit uptight? Does one of you seem to be the nag in the relationship, always upset about little things, while the other seems to be in a defensive mode most of the time? For my wife and I, the answers to these questions are "yes!" "yes!" and "yes!" And if your answers are the same, this book is a must-read.

Eliminating the Gender Factor
(*It's What Makes This Book Different*)

Most books about marriage are based on gender. They talk about the differences between the sexes and suggest ways to help manage those differences. I have found these books to be helpful, but they usually leave me in a bit of a

7

dilemma. I related more to the ladies' section than I did to the men's! For example, when I read Dr. John Gray's best-selling *Men are from Mars and Women are from Venus*, I was more from Venus than from Mars. In *His Needs, Her Needs*, by Willard F. Harley Jr., I had far more of *her* needs that I had of *his*.

Wow! Am I weird or what? To find out if I am, I went on a journey of discovery. What I found out on that journey led me to write this book, but before we get into it, I need to make something perfectly clear: my identification with the ladies' sections in those books was strictly in the area of *personality* differences and needs, not *sexuality*. On this point, let's be clear. When it comes to sex, I am totally male and my wife Valencia is absolutely female. What more can I say? We are so in love in every way.

Well, having said that, let's go back to my little "problem" with gender-based books. Now, no doubt, they probably work for about 80% of marriages. But what about the other 20%? The guys like me who line up on the female personality side, or ladies who are over there with the male personality traits? Figuring there had to be an explanation, I began my search for a concept that eliminates the gender factor, one that would impact that 20% (and probably many in the other 80%). Well, with the Lord's help, I believe I have found that concept. It's called personality chemistry.

Do you realize that that every couple has a personality chemistry? It is a powerful, dynamic chemistry, one that is uniquely expressed by and through the husband and wife couple, united as one in the marriage relationship. The chemistry is designed to produce ever-increasing growth in a marriage, year after year. But there is a downside. When the chemistry is mishandled or ignored, vicious cycles of conflict result. If left unchecked, these cycles harm and ultimately destroy marriages.

So, what you have in your hand is more than just a manual listing personality labels. It is a powerful tool that will make you aware of your marriage's personality chemistry, and give you down-to-earth, practical ways to manage it.

If you feel that you are in a marriage like mine—one of extreme, possibly irreconcilable opposites—by all means read on!

Pastor Ken Peters
Covenant Church Spokane
Spokane, Washington

Section 1

Discovery

Discovery

Without Faith and Commitment
it is Impossible

I don't believe a marriage book can work for you unless you have *faith* for your marriage and *commitment* to your vows. This book is primarily for couples that are building their marriage on those two values. Without faith and commitment, the practical principles that you will discover in this book will simply not work over the long term. Faith and commitment are the foundation. The principles are the framework.

Faith. As you know, the Bible has much to say about faith. Without faith, it is impossible to please God. With faith, we can move mountains. Well, marriage is full of mountains to move. It is full of challenges. Without faith you simply will not succeed. You have to keep believing for a great marriage or you won't get it. With faith, all things are possible. The reverse is also true ... without faith, nothing is possible.

Jesus said oftentimes, "According to your faith, be it unto you." What a statement of absolute truth! Your marriage will end up being "according to *your* faith." Now, of course, in a marriage there are two, so, according to both spouses' faith, be it unto them.

Commitment. Commitment is a very important by-product of faith. Commitment means keeping our promises even though we don't feel like it ... when we don't feel in love ... when we don't feel faith. Those are the times when we must *remember* our words, our vows, our promises, *and* be careful to perform them. We must remember that we said, "For better or for worse," and then keep that promise. No doubt, promises are easier to say than perform. For that reason, it is essential that we place a high value on commitment, or loyalty, to our words and to our promises.

Referring to one's personal life, Jesus once said that a house that is built on sand will collapse when the storm comes. The same is true of your marriage. Your home will not stand if you don't build on the Rock, Jesus Christ.

How do you build on the Rock? Through the timeless principles of faith and commitment. If these two values are not in place, you will be trying to build on a faulty foundation. Please remember that as you continue in this book.

The Skin and Skeleton Concept

When a designer creates a line of clothing, the products in the line tend to look the same. Take designer Tommy Hilfiger, for example. Or Ralph Lauren. All of their clothes have a certain look. You can hold two different pieces of clothing and both of them have that look. The same is true of the creations made by the Great Designer, God. As different as His creations are, we can see in them a common thread, or theme.

Take our bodies and minds, for example. God designed them, and as different as they appear to be from one another, they are actually much the same.

Let's begin with the body. As far as body structure is concerned, we are made of skin and bones. We recognize this fact when we say about a person who has very little fat, "He/she is just skin and bones." This shows that our basic body framework and structure are skin and bones.

Now consider the mind. I believe God made our minds with the same structural ideas with which He made our bodies. Just as our bodies have skin and bones, so too do our minds. The skeleton in our mind provides sturdiness and boundaries while the skin covers the bones, providing beauty and defense. The skin and skeleton of our minds deal with the mental world, just as the skin and skeleton of our bodies deal with the physical world.

When God created man, He created him in His image. This means that man was complete in every area of his tripartite (three-part) being. His spirit, his soul and his body were all made holy. "Holy" comes from the root word "whole," which means perfect or complete. Thus, at the time of the Genesis creation, man was completely holy, that is, he was without sin or shortcomings of any kind in his spirit, soul, and body.

As we know, Adam chose to sin. This was a disaster of cataclysmic proportions because the results of his sin — death and sinfulness—were passed on to us. Because he lost his holiness, so did we. Because he lost his perfect structure, so did we. Because his spirit (the eternal part) died, so did ours (to be brought back to life only through faith in Jesus Christ). Man's mind—no longer sinless, perfect, and holy—became a mere fraction of what it was in its perfect condition. With his spirit dead and his soul and body in decay, it was clear that man would no longer live forever, as God intended.

Because man's mind shrank to a fraction of its original holiness, or perfection, we are now born with only portions of our mental skin and skeleton. Some people have more skeleton than skin and some have more skin than skeleton. Everyone has different portions. I was born with a lot of skeleton, and my little sister Barbie was born with a lot of skin. My mom has a lot of skeleton, and my dad has a lot of skin. These unequal portions created chemistry in my home as I grew up. Some of it was good, some bad.

When we get married, we marry spouses who have percentages of mental skin and skeleton that are different from ourselves. The result is a chemistry that we are left to deal with. When the spouses are extreme opposites, the chemistry becomes very evident in the home, especially in my home. You see, my wife is what I call "an extreme Skin," while I am just the opposite—"an extreme Skeleton."

Wow, you should have seen the chemistry in action after our honeymoon was over! We laugh about it today, but some of those vicious cycles I mentioned earlier were obvious, everyday, and tough to reverse. But, thank God, through the principles in this book we were able to "reverse the curse," and put a stop to those havoc-wreaking tornadoes.

You and your spouse, or your spouse to be, may not be as opposite as Val and I are, but be ready. You will definitely confront some chemistry problems and vicious cycles to one degree or another. But right now, let's look at this skin and skeleton concept from a Biblical perspective.

The first reference occurs in Genesis 2:23 when God made Eve from Adam's rib: "This is now *bone* of my *bones* and *flesh* of my *flesh.*" Paul repeated the concept in Ephesians 5:30: "For we are members of His body, of His *flesh* and of His *bones.*" Notice that both of these references—one in the Old Testament and one in the New Testament—mention flesh and bones in the context of marriage.

Let's not make the mistake of thinking that Adam and Paul were speaking only of physical union. I believe that, in Ephesians 5:30, Paul considered the mental skin and skeleton to be factors in the union. As proof of this, consider what happens when two people divorce. Divorce takes place first in the mental arena, then the physical. To be sure, as married human beings, we need our spouse to complete us in the physical skin and skeleton aspect, but (and this is essential for success in every area of marriage) we must realize that God's Word includes our mental skin and skeleton in that completion.

In both Genesis and Ephesians, the Bible makes it clear that the two are to become one, both physically and mentally. This meshing of bones and flesh is the goal of this book. In particular, I want to help you and your spouse become one *mentally*. To go from different, separate portions of mental flesh and bones to a joined entity where the fruit of the Spirit abounds. So, get ready for elevation! And let me prophesy the Word of God over you right now. "The two of you shall become one, in Jesus' Name!"

Opposites Attract at First and Then ...

We've all heard the term, "Opposites attract." This is true in so many cases, and I know, for sure, that it was true in my life. As I grew up, it was never the dominant, bossy girls that I was attracted to. It was the easy-going, relaxed ones. As a result, behold! Valencia—the queen of easy-going and relaxed, and strong in it! The moment I met her and sensed her spirit, I decided that I was going to marry her. The rest is history. We are now building a great family together—even though we could not be more opposite in personality. We share the same values, hold the same doctrines, and dream the same dreams—even though she is my extreme opposite. Somehow (*how did it happen?*), we were mysteriously attracted to each other.

Actually, I think it's humorous to see how many couples are made up of extremely opposite personalities. And it must be a natural phenomenon, a subconscious attraction thing, because we don't even know it is going on! I mean, I never knew why I was attracted to a certain kind of female and not another, no matter their level of physical beauty. All I knew is—I was attracted!

I believe it is an attraction that God puts into place. Here's how it works. Very simple. The reason you are so attracted to an opposite personality is this: your mind was looking for its missing part. The dominant skeleton mind was looking for some skin and the dominant skin mind was looking for some skeleton. I guess the term "Soul Mate" is an accurate one. Your mind is a part of your soul, along with your will and your emotions. So, when your mind finds what it's missing, your soul has found its mate. In my case, I can tell you for sure—Valencia is truly my soul mate.

After you find your soul mate, experience the honeymoon, and have been married for a year or two, the same factors that brought you together begin to become your problem. In my case, I began to view the easy-going personality that first attracted me to my wife as unawareness and a lack of consideration. My confidence and on-top-of-it personality became, for Val, an attitude of superiority and nagging. Soon we were swirling in a vicious cycle of offense and defense. In an attempt to stop her from being defensive, I became more aggressive. For her part, to counter my increased aggressiveness, she became even more laid back! Of course, this worked like a charm (yeah, sure). So, bottom line, what had attracted me at first was now my pet peeve. *And this is usually what happens when opposites marry.*

When marriage happens, a grafting takes place. The Bible says that the two become one. In wedding ceremonies, we light candles to symbolize the joining of flesh and bone in one. Adam said that Eve became bone of his bone and flesh of his flesh. The skin and the skeleton are grafted together by a surgery of God called marriage. The grafting "takes" at first and then, after the honeymoon, at some point down the road, the two entities begin to repel. The grafting just doesn't seem to work. At that point, to ensure that the grafting will "take" again, the two must decide to turn to God for wisdom, knowledge, and discretion—resources that you will find in the coming pages.

The Danger of Becoming a Halloween Decoration

Opposites naturally attract at first and then begin to repel. Rather than trying to circumvent or reject this principle in marriage, we should accept it as a natural sequence, one we can learn from and grow through. Trust the Lord that He has a purpose for it. And realize too that, obviously, His purpose is not divorce. The Bible is clear that He hates divorce because of the pain it causes every member of the family.

Some matchmaking companies have adopted the philosophy of hooking up people who are similar instead of opposite, so the odds of a successful marriage will increase. That just may be true. Couples with the same personality may have a high success rate.

When it comes to sameness, I do think that we should marry someone with the same basic values, belief system, and dreams. But I believe couples miss out on the glory that comes from marrying and growing with an opposite. It's my belief that God had a plan when He built into us an attraction for the opposite. I am so glad a matchmaking company didn't hook me up with someone just like me. How boring that would be! I am convinced that it would have left large areas of my life undeveloped and devoid of fruitfulness.

I believe that God, the Master Matchmaker, put what I call an "attraction magnet" into mankind. He purposely uses the magnet to "trick" us into marrying an extreme opposite. And for what purpose? To put us into a situation that forces us to grow in holiness. Hey, we think we are getting married for happiness, but hold on; the Lord has a different idea.

His reason for us getting married is holiness. Nothing will make or break you or give you the chance to grow like marrying an opposite personality that doesn't understand you and that you don't understand. Marriage to an opposite gives the skeleton a chance to put on more skin, and gives the skin a chance to cover more bones.

A common goal that devoted Christians have for themselves is to become more like Jesus. In recent years, many took to wearing bracelets with the initials W.W.J.D. which means, "What would Jesus Do?" This expresses a sincere desire to become more and more like the Savior, Jesus Christ. Growing up in church, I used to sing a song entitled, *Lord, I want to be more like You.* Another song spoke of a deep longing for holiness. We Christians pray for holiness, we sing about it, and I believe God answered our prayer when He led us into marriage with our spouse. I believe when we pray, "Lord, help me to be more like you," He turns to us and says, "Then look at your spouse and become more like them."

Failing to use marriage to an opposite as a way to holiness puts us in danger of becoming a Halloween decoration. Think about it. How about those skinless skeletons hanging in store windows? Or the ones propped up in front yards to scare people? Skeletons that do not evolve are scary individuals, and they stay that way too. I think we've all known a scary skeleton that is so abrasive or grumpy that we cringe when they head our way. (Pray that they are in a good mood that day.) And how about a skin without bones? Looks like a ghost, right? Ghosts are also used to bring the fear factor at Halloween—floppy and sneaky. That's what Skins become when they do not develop bones. Hey, you know what? I am determined not to end up like a Halloween decoration. I deeply desire to grow in the areas that need growth. I desperately want to evolve into a great personality by patching my weaknesses and soaring with my strengths. My marriage (yes, to my extreme opposite) gives me a chance to do just that!

Conflict: The Opportunity to Grow

Dealing with conflict is a major part of this book. You will be learning not only how to resolve it successfully but also how to prevent it. So, before we go on, let's put conflict into its proper perspective.

First of all, we should not be afraid of conflict. Conflict is not a horrible word. No, conflict is not enjoyable, but it has a purpose. And don't conclude that if you experience a lot of conflict in your marriage that you are incompatible, or that you have irreconcilable differences. If that were the case, my wife and I would be done for. But we aren't. On the contrary, it may seem hard to believe, but we have learned to regard conflict as our friend—if we use it properly.

Conflict is an opportunity for personal growth. If you didn't have conflict with anyone there would be no reason for you to change in any way. Without conflict you would never even be aware that there was a problem with you or the other person. Remember the movie *Cast Away* starring Tom Hanks as an airplane crash survivor on a desert island? Halfway through the movie, Hanks finds a volleyball, draws a face on it, and names it Mr. Wilson. Hanks' relationship to

Mr. Wilson added warmth and humor to Hanks' desperate situation, but because "he" was not alive, Mr. Wilson could not create any conflict with Hanks. Therefore he could not help Hanks grow as a character in this movie. We need contact with people other than Mr. Wilson. "Iron sharpens iron," the Bible teaches. This means that people who spend time together create conflict, and that conflict shows us how we should change. Yes, of course, conflict is not the only way to grow. So, we don't want to encourage conflict. But we must recognize its importance in the growth process. When conflict shows up, think of it as a sign that we need to grow together, not separate what God has put together.

Finally, in dealing with marital conflict, we must have the mindset that neither spouse is right or wrong, just different. Avoid that spirit of self-righteousness at all cost. It will destroy you and your marriage relationship. Instead, understand that both individuals tend to think that their way of dealing with the world is the right way. The easy-going one thinks that avoiding conflict is right, while the uptight one insists on dealing with it as it comes. The easy-going one thinks the marriage is bad if you *are* dealing with conflict all the time, while the uptight one feels that the marriage is bad if you *aren't* constantly dealing with conflict. So, which one is right and which one is wrong? Answer? Both are usually right and both are usually wrong in every situation. More on this up ahead ...

The Test: Who Plays What Part in Your Marriage?

One of the best known of the many paradoxical statements found in the Bible is this one written by Paul the Apostle: "When I am weak, then I am strong." Here is my expanded version of it: the more I am aware of my weaknesses and am humble enough to admit them, I become stronger and stronger. Before I can adjust, negotiate and evolve with my spouse, I must first recognize what my natural strengths and weaknesses are. I can then begin to utilize and maximize my strength while at the same time acknowledging and mending my weaknesses.

I should note right here that life is complex. We are all at different places in our personal growth and in our stages of life. Because no two individuals are the same, I don't want to oversimplify marriage issues. Yet, at the same time, there are similarities in marriage chemistry for many folks. Therefore, in order to help you, this book aims to share the lessons my wife and I are learning as we learn to negotiate our differences.

Let's start with this incontrovertible fact: The person in our life that is easiest to deceive is you. This usually plays out this way: people want to be the person that they are not. We tend to want to be what other people are—especially the ones that possess our weakness as their strength. As you begin to figure out which side of the fence you are on, be very careful to be realistic (not idealistic) about who you are. The sooner you are humble enough to accept who you are, the sooner God will exalt you. You can't find your way and make progress with the help of a map until you locate where the *You are Here* place. My goal here is neither to label you nor give you an excuse to stay where you are. I want to give you a chance to grow. Accurate understanding gives you a chance to be wise. Inaccurate understanding keeps you trapped in the place where you are. So keep an open mind as we begin:

SMOKE SCREENS

We are about to find out who is a Skin and who is a Skeleton, but before we begin, we need to recognize what I call "smoke screens." Smoke screens are personality attributes that are NOT factors in identifying your self:

1. **Introvert and extrovert** have nothing to do with your being a Skin or Skeleton. I know many introverts and extroverts of both kinds.

2. **Gender** is not a factor. It seems that most women are Skeletons. But not me. I am an example of a male Skeleton married to a female Skin.

   PERSONAL NOTE: *I do find it interesting that God made woman out of a rib (a skeletal part) and that most women are Skeletons. Most gender-based marriage books assume that the man is the Skin and that the woman is the Skeleton. You will recall that I wrote this book because gender-based books always put me in the female category. I believe this book eliminates the gender problem found in most marriage materials.*

3. Neither category is **Most Likely to Succeed**. I

have seen great leaders from both categories. Success and leadership are partly given to the ones who play to their strength and mend their weaknesses.

4. **A Bad Temper** is not a determining factor. There are temper-losing Skins and temper-losing Skeletons. Skeletons often heat up about the little things more quickly, but when it comes down to it, both Skin and Skeleton are subject to fits of rage.

5. Neither personality is **more right** or **more wrong**. They are just different.

6. Neither personality is **more neat and tidy** or **organized** than the other. Skins tend to be more tidy and routine while Skeletons are more organized and prioritized, but this is not always the case.

7. Neither one is more **on time** than the other. This is just a character issue that can be developed by either.

8. Neither one is **more sensitive** than the other. Skeletons often appear really tough due to their natural abrasiveness, but oftentimes they are more sensitive than Skins.

9. Neither one is **more rude** than the other. They just have different types of rudeness. Skins can come across as really snotty and arrogant. Skeletons seem to create conflict when irritated.

SKIN TEST—SKELETON TEST

The following are questions and keys that will help you determine the part you play in your marriage: Dominant Skeleton? Or dominant Skin? As you proceed, keep in mind that you may play one part in your marriage and a different part in another relationship. Try to focus strictly on your marriage relationship.

1. If someone lived in your home for five years, which one would they consider the nag? ... Silent or not, the nag in the relationship is probably the **Skeleton**.

2. Which one feels like the other person should just relax and get off their back? ... This person is probably the **Skin**.

3. Which one seems to be irritated at the other first about little things? Who seems to be always upset about something? Who seems more likely to be the one making mountains out of molehills? ... This person is probably the **Skeleton**.

4. Which one wishes that the other person would relax, enjoy life a little, let some stuff go, and quit making a big deal about every little thing ... This person is probably the **Skin**.

5. Which one can't stand any inconvenience, gets totally bent out of shape and creates massive conflict if they feel that the inconvenience could have been prevented by their spouse? ... This person

is probably the **Skeleton**.

6. Which one has more patience, and doesn't get "bent out of shape" about spilled milk? This one feels that these things are just a part of life, and cannot be prevented. In fact, they feel that trying to prevent these little things will drive them crazy ... This person is probably the **Skin**.

7. Which of you has the harder time forgiving because you don't think the other is being sincere in the apology? You feel like they are just trying to sweep it under the carpet ... They don't really want to learn the lesson from this problem ... This person is probably the **Skeleton**.

8. Which one says things like this? *Get over it already! After all, I've said, 'I'm sorry.' Do you have to keep rubbing this in? It's done! What do you want me to do about it? All I can do is apologize... would you let it go?* ... This person is probably the **Skin**.

9. Which one feels that if they don't make it happen, it won't get done? He/she is the Creator of The Honey-Do List, the one that makes sure things get crossed off. He/she is the one who holds the other accountable; who makes sure that the other isn't slacking off. ... This person is probably the **Skeleton**.

10. Which one feels like, *If they don't get off my back, it'll never get done!? I'll do it when I get to it, and if they have a problem with that they can do it themselves.*

... This person is probably the **Skin**.

11. Which one seems to be more concerned about family time? That their spouse doesn't manage their time well by making time for what matters? ... This person is probably the **Skeleton**.

12. Which one enjoys independence—being able to go wherever they want, whenever they want? Which one feels that by having to report in on everything they are being treated like a child? (And you didn't get married so you could have a new MOM or a DAD!!!) ... This person is probably the **Skin**.

13. Which one feels like the other should just know what to do and what to say at the right time without being told? *After all, if they really cared about me, they would know what to do by now. They should know how I like sex, they should know what kind of soda I like, and they should know what I would like for my birthday. If they really loved me, they would know, etc, etc., etc.* This person doesn't learn and doesn't listen ... This person is probably the **Skeleton**.

14. Which one feels that it is unrealistic for the other person to expect them to read their mind? *If they want something, they should ask nicely. Just be nice and maybe they will get what they want* ... This person is probably the **Skin**.

15. Which one feels that the other is unthoughtful, inconsiderate, and oblivious? *Why is he/she so*

unaware of my needs and my plans? He/she gets so consumed with whatever person or situation is grabbing for their attention, instead of keeping me in mind ... This person is probably the **Skeleton**.

16. Which one feels that the other is way too aware, too controlling, too tracking everything they do or don't do? ... This person is probably the **Skin**.

17. Which one feels that the other just doesn't listen? *They just shut me off when I'm talking. They don't learn. They are so defensive, and things will never get any better in this relationship* ...This person is probably the **Skeleton**.

18. Which one feels that the other should stop trying to teach them the lesson and just leave them to God? *If they would talk nicely, and treat me with respect, maybe I would listen* ... This person is probably the **Skin**.

19. Which one wants to make sure that the other person learns the lesson from every situation so that this particular problem will never, never, never happen again. *And until they understand everything about what happened, and how to prevent it next time, I cannot forgive* ... This person is probably the **Skeleton**.

20. Which one feels that the other person should learn how to forgive, to let things go, and not try to prevent future situations right now? *There is no way to prevent everything!* ... This person is probably

the **Skin.**

21. Which one feels that the other is too independent in the money area, and doesn't check in with you before making decisions on plans and finances? ... This person is probably the **Skeleton.**

22. Which one feels that the other should trust you and give you the freedom to live and spend money as they wish ... This person is probably the **Skin.**

23. Which one tends to get more and more angry and abrasive in their approach when they get hurt or frustrated? ... This person is probably the **Skeleton.**

24. When feeling hurt and frustrated, which one tends to get numb, distant, and icy—tending to hold things in until all heck breaks loose? ... This person is probably the **Skin.**

25. Which one feels that conflict should be managed and problems taken care of as they come up, and that this type of communication is the key to a great relationship? ... This person is probably the **Skeleton**

26. Which one feels that if they always have to be managing conflict then the relationship is bad? ... This person is probably the **Skin.**

27. Which one seems to be the constantly stressed-out one? ... This person is probably the **Skeleton.**

28. Which one seems to be more easy-going? ... This
    person is probably the **Skin**.

I hope that this test has created some real clarity about
the part you play in your marriage. The rest of this book will
not be as effective as it could be if you don't know who you
are.

NOTE: Some of these questions could go opposite ways
for you. If that is the case, go back and reread questions 1-4.
Your answers to the first four questions are the most defini-
tive and revealing of all.

So, do you know what part you play in your marriage?
Good! Now that you know who you are, you can begin to
learn how to manage the differences. God bless you as you
continue!

The Vicious Cycle

Television producers make millions off the Skin and Skeleton chemistry. *Everybody Loves Raymond*, *King of Queens* and
According to Jim are just a few of the many TV comedies with
Skin husbands and Skeleton wives. The guy is the easy-going, amorous, fun-loving, oblivious one—always making
mistakes and then trying to cover them up by lying or going
on the defensive. The wife, with all the force of her skeletal,
common sense mind, tries (usually in vain) to control her
independent, oblivious husband. She holds him accountable,
catches him in his sin, and then, when he tries to cover up,
catches him in his lie. It should be no surprise that these
shows rake in so much money and are on the air for years

and years. Their true-to-life characters and scenarios keep audiences in stitches week after week.

Sadly, the issues played out for fun on TV aren't quite so funny when they are the stuff of real life for viewers. In real life, the trivialized, petty issues of TV create a world of hurt, frustration and confusion. They are vicious cycles, wreaking short-term and long-term havoc in the hearts and lives of families across the land. These cycles, offensive and defensive, go on and on for days, weeks, months, and years. Unless they are reversed, they can cripple what might otherwise have been a healthy, flourishing relationship.

Have you heard the statement, "We get upset about the stupidest little things"? Actually, it's not the little issue that is the problem. It is the vicious cycle that is created around that little issue. It is the attacking spirit of the Skeleton and the defensive spirit of the Skin that together creates that tornado and keeps it in motion.

Hurricanes and tornadoes exist because of forces in our global weather system. The same is true in marriage. In the globe of our marriage, the chemistry between the Skin and the Skeleton creates hurricanes and tornadoes. These tornadoes can destroy neighborhoods and towns in our relationships. These destructive cycles are actually chains of reactions in one person that trigger reactions in the other person. The reactions go back and forth between the two, getting worse and worse, until they are finally reversed. Therefore each home must have a well-developed tornado watch system. If we quickly become aware of them and understand what is happening to create these vicious cycles, then we can do the opposite in order to slow down and eventually reverse them.

When a tornado is spotted, someone needs to sound the alarm. *Honey, we are in a vicious cycle right now!* Sin dwells in darkness and shining a light on sin is half the battle. Being aware of actions and reactions gives us a chance to be wise. But if you don't first understand, you don't even have a shot at being wise. So, in order to know how to reverse cycles, we need to identify them. Break down the word "understand." When you get the "under," then you have an opportunity to "stand." When you stand and do the right thing at the right time, the decision is called wisdom. For every bad cycle and any bad chemistry problem, there is an antibiotic. First identify the infection and bad chemistry, and then take the right antibiotic.

Here is a blow-by-blow account of the most common of all vicious cycles:

1. Both are living their normal lives with their moods and circumstances varying from day to day.

2. The Skin unintentionally irritates, frustrates or hurts the Skeleton by doing something wrong or by not doing something right.

3. The Skeleton feels irritated, frustrated or hurt and lets the Skin know about it.

4. The Skin feels disrespected, dishonored, and disliked.

5. The Skin does not receive the communication or correction because of the Skeleton's abrasiveness.

6. The Skin becomes defensive and reveals this

34

spirit by making some remark or facial expression, or by becoming non-responsive.

7. The Skeleton feels angrier than before and turns into a prosecuting attorney. The Skin has just invalidated his/her irritation, and now it must be proven logically that his/her frustration is valid. The Skeleton tries to make a case that will convict the Skin. The Skeleton may intensify the attack or get very passive aggressive, both of which are very abrasive to the Skin. Under the Skeleton's verbal barrage, the Skin's character is methodically torn down. The impassioned Skeleton makes his/her case by claiming that this mistake is the same old one the Skin has been making for the last ten years. The Skin is made to understand just how stubborn, stupid, non-integral, and immature he/she really is. If the Skin walks away, the Skeleton is sure to follow — wherever the Skin goes so the Skin does not get away with this awful crime.

8. Now the Skin gets more defensive, accusing the Skeleton of something off the beaten track just a little to fluster and confuse the Skeleton. He/she explains that the offence was unintentional, unintended. Reasons are given which make complete sense to the Skin. Outgoing Skins may lose their tempers just to back the Skeleton off, and get off their case. Introvert Skins may pretend to listen and be sorry. They may fake understanding,

give the impression of false humility, offer a phony apology, and inwardly celebrate their having played that stupid Skeleton like a fiddle. They will take a loss and play the martyr, or just walk away and leave the room to get the Skeleton off their back.

To be honest, Valencia and I have allowed this cycle to access our home all too often. One instance really stands out — Thanksgiving Day, 2004:

I love Thanksgiving. I love the whole family, food and football thing (I get to watch my second favorite team, the Dallas Cowboys). Also, a nice plus about Thanksgiving is the leftovers that I get to munch on for about a week afterwards. For best results, I ask Val to put extra gravy and cranberry sauce in the pantry to load on to the leftover turkey and dressing for the next few days.

Well, on this particular holiday, I asked Valencia to buy four cans of cranberry sauce — one for Thanksgiving night and three for leftovers. My wife did exactly what I asked — at first. She bought the four cans of cranberries and brought them home. Unfortunately, though, instead of putting the extra cans in the pantry, she (absent-mindedly, she told me later) opened all of them on Thanksgiving night!

Now, these were the jellied type of cranberries, and looking back, it is kind of funny and cute, but she put them on a plate and wrapped them in saran wrap (which proved to be incredibly inconvenient). First of all, putting this plate with floating cranberries into a fridge already jam-packed with holiday goodies, etc. made for a frustrating situation every time you went on a leftover turkey search. Then, once I did find some and attempted to put cranberries on the turkey and dressing the saran wrap was incredibly slimy and irritating to peel away from the oozing cranberry jelly. And, as you can imagine, re-wrapping that liquefied mess was even worse.

Now, if I had used common sense, I would have put the cranberries in a plastic container, and the situation would have been a done deal. But, no, I kept using the system that was in place, and got more and more irritated every day. Finally, after three days of frustration, I could keep silent no longer. Valencia was in the kitchen as I was digging out some leftovers, so I said,

Did you open up all the cranberry sauces? This was a rude question because, of course, she had opened them all.

Yeah. To her it was no big deal. What difference did it make? Typical Skin, right?

Oh, but to me this was a big deal! I wait all year for turkey leftovers and cranberry sauce. I love cranberry sauce in the pantry, and in a can! It doesn't make any sense to me to open them all at once.

Why did you wrap this in saran wrap? As you can well imagine this made her feel even more defensive. It went downhill from there.

My voice and temperature rising and skin color deepening, I began to tell my dear wife how I felt.

You don't even like cranberry sauce, so what's it to you? You don't care if I have to peel slimy saran wrap off the cranberries, and fumble around with this awkward arrangement every time I open the fridge. How dare you be smart-mouthed and defensive with me?

Well, dear reader, I had lost my cool, hadn't I? About ten minutes later, when the dust cleared, I apologized for talking in an arrogant tone of voice and for losing my cool. Valencia apologized for not thinking the cranberry sauce through better, and for being defensive.

The above situation, with its conversation and chain of actions and reactions, is typical of the vicious cycles we need to be on the lookout for in our homes. An offensive-defensive cycle can go on and on for days and weeks and months within marriages. If it is not reversed, it can cripple what could have been a happy life together.

Four Levels of Dealing with Marriage Conflict

This book is about successfully dealing with conflict, about using conflict for our benefit. Your success in marriage does not depend on a couple avoiding conflict. Rather, it hinges on both people having the ability to deal with it. Both husband and wife must play together as a team for conflict resolution to be a success. The solutions presented in this book will only work for couples that sincerely desire to do so.

The four levels of dealing with marriage conflict are as follows:

1. No Resolution

On this level, a couple just learns to live with conflict, satisfied to leave it unresolved. Couples on this level resort to making sarcastic put-down remarks to each other. Such remarks are enough victory for them. They push their dissonant feelings aside and continue to get on with life. They have signed a marriage certificate, but they just exist together.

2. Rough Resolution

Things are said in anger that shouldn't be said. Volume levels are high, insults are hurled. Problems are worked out, but damage is done to each person in the process. There are plenty of things to apologize for once the argument is over. Someone watching the disagreement would definitely think that this couple has a problem.

3. Team Resolution

Level three couples are good at resolving conflicts. Working as teams, they learn how to resolve them quickly and smoothly without damage to either person. On this level, conflicts are more like molehills than mountains. Yes, there are times when lengthy discussions are required, but for the most part, problems are minimal and dealt with appropriately. The "little things" no longer create those vicious cycles. (Most couples do not reach level three. If you move into level three, you will be one of the few.)

4. Prevention

On level four, couples not only smoothly resolve conflict, they prevent much of it. Now, living on planet earth means conflict-free marriage is impossible. But preventing a good portion of it can move couples into a level of happiness and love that most only dream of. This is the level where husband and wife are usually happy together, really enjoying one another. The environment and spirit of the marriage flourish with the fruit of the Spirit: love, joy, peace, longsuffering, gentleness, goodness, and temperance. Key to the success of such couples is their commitment to work hard, to suppress their fleshly inclinations, and to make personality adjustments.

At this point, I need to issue a strong caution. Many people are completely frustrated with their marriage. They feel like giving up. One reason for this is that they are trying to get to level four without going through level three. I see this all the time in my pastoring and counseling. The best advice I can give is this: do not try to skip level three. Tackling level four when you aren't on level three will frustrate you to no end, and even make you feel like quitting. Instead, if you will focus on level three for five years, you will find that level four will happen almost automatically.

Level three means a happy home. Level three is the key to making it to fifty years. Level three means that your kids will grow up knowing that mom and dad are crazy about each other. So, let God move you into level four. Go through the proper process that God has called you to walk through.

Section 2

Cure

Cure

Need and Weakness Cycle # 1

In Ephesians 5:33, Paul the Apostle tells us that husbands should love their wives, and that wives should respect their husbands. This has to happen in order for flesh and bones to come together. For the sake of the Skin and Skeleton concept, let me paraphrase this verse: *Skin, love your Skeleton spouse. Skeleton, respect your Skin spouse.*

To reverse cycles, you first have to identify them. Let's begin with Weakness and Need Cycle #1. This cycle occurs when the **primary weakness** of one party prevents the **primary need** of the other from being fulfilled. Reversing it results in a curing of present conflict.

The **primary need** of the Skin is to feel liked and respected by the Skeleton. Feeling liked and respected is oxygen for a Skin's soul. When a good supply of the oxygen is not there, their soul begins to suffocate. They then grasp for air any way that they can get it. In fact, they don't care about anything else until they first have this need met. They must first be able to breathe before they can think. This is a need that must be filled on a regular basis.

The **primary weakness** of the Skeleton is being kind and respectful when feeling irritated, frustrated, or hurt by the Skin. And feeling that way is not difficult for them—they often make mountains out of molehills, have a hard time controlling their emotions, and are not good at seasoning their speech with grace. Also, because Skeletons tend to wear their feelings on their sleeve, they make lousy actors, fakers, and hypocrites. Being kind and respectful, or even acting that way, is the last thing on their mind.

So, do you see the problem? The Skin needs respect, and the Skeleton has a horrible time being respectful when upset in any way. The Skin needs to feel liked and it's nearly impossible for the Skeleton to be kind when feeling hurt or irritated. This is the #1 Need/Weakness Cycle, the one that causes us so much trouble and conflict.

Summary

1. The primary need of the Skin is to feel liked and respected by the Skeleton.

2. The greatest weakness of the Skeleton is being kind and respectful when feeling irritated, frustrated, or hurt.

Curing Present Conflict (CPC): The Main Skeleton Key

Skeletons, this is for you. If you understand nothing else in this book, understand the key I am about to give you, and put it to use every once in a while. If you do, your chance of success in marriage to a Skin is great.

Skeletons, you are abrasive by nature. This is especially true when you are feeling irritated, frustrated, or hurt by Skins (which may be often). The main character quality you need to develop is the ability to be kind and respectful—right in the midst of your upset condition. Not an easy thing to do, but developing that ability is the most important and needful thing you can use as the key to curing present conflict.

Do you want to live out this key? First of all, then, recognize that doing so is impossible without God's love and help. Any success I have had with this key is because of Him. But there was a time when I thought it was impossible for me. And here's why: We extrovert Skeletons pride ourselves in being honest and transparent. We are proud that no one ever has to wonder if we are happy or not. We consider ourselves to be "black-and-white people"—proud of saying what we mean and meaning what we say. Having opinions, we appreciate living in America where our opinions can be voiced. Introvert Skeletons feel the same way. They tend to keep their feelings inside for the most part, but you can still tell whether or not they are happy.

As you know, when the Skeleton feels hurt by the Skin, the last thing on his mind is making sure that the Skin feels liked and respected. In fact, everything in their nature wants to do the opposite. Skeletons feel that respect should be earned by their spouse and if, in their judgment, it isn't, then they don't want to give it out for free. Skeletons have a hard time showing like and respect externally when they are feeling disdain internally. Instead of bestowing compliments and good feelings, they are more likely to offer "constructive" criticism—letting the Skin know that they don't approve of the Skin's misbehavior.

Here is a case in point. When Valencia and I went to Hawaii for a pastor's conference and our 10th anniversary, we had a situation come up, one that I found to be very enlightening. After visiting Pearl Harbor, we were driving to the north shore of Oahu. As we conversed, there was something about Val's responses that I felt was impolite and improper. It was about the third time it had happened that day, so by now I was hurt and frustrated. But I knew that if I said something at this point, I would not say it in the right way. So I internalized my hurt and got quiet. Well, Valencia noticed that I was upset, and, thinking to herself, "What Now?" she asked me, "What's the Matter?"

Given the opportunity, I began to share with her in what I thought was a mild-mannered, gentle way. But, to my surprise, she became defensive and non-understanding. Now I was really frustrated, because I thought that I had handled myself fairly well.

"Valencia," I asked in exasperation, "what am I supposed to do with my hurt? If I say it nice and you don't receive it, how am I going to get this resolved?"

Then, this idea came to me. Why not ask her to put herself in your shoes, and show you how to make it palatable so that she could receive it with meekness. So, I did just that. And, you know, she came back with some information. It was very wise information, but it also shook me up! She told me that she didn't feel like I liked her, and she wanted to feel liked. She felt that I despised her and disrespected her to the core. She said that I should let her know that I liked her as a person before telling her about what she did. She also said that I should put boundaries around the thing that she did by saying, "This is only one thing about you out of about 500 things that I am having a problem with ... I love the other 499 things."

You know what? That conversation was life changing and very revealing to me about Skin nature.

Skeletons, in your quest for the love of your Skin spouse, memorize and live by these key Scripture verses:

▸ Ephesians 4:15. "Speak the truth in love."
▸ Ephesians 4:26. "Be angry and sin not."
▸ Colossians 4:6. "Let your speech be always seasoned with grace."
▸ Mark 9:23. "All things are possible to those who believe." (Probably the most important of all.)

In his book, *The Seven Habits of Highly Effective People*, Steve Covey teaches that between every stimulus and response there is an area of freedom. In this space of freedom we have the ability to choose our action or reaction. None of us have to be victims of the negative stimulus given to us. That is what the scripture, *Be angry and sin not*, means. It is not wrong to feel the stimulus of anger, but it is wrong to act in an angry way that is not productive.

Don't make the mistake of thinking that your angry re-action produces only short-term results. I can tell you from experience that the Bible is right in saying that fits of rage do not produce the righteousness of Christ. While it is not wrong for the Skeleton to feel irritated, frustrated or hurt, it is not a license to behave wrongfully. It is sinful to react in an unkind and disrespectful way towards the Skin when a negative stimulus is received. Do the right thing. Use your space of freedom to respond kindly and respectfully.

Summary

1. For Skeletons, this is a most important, but diffi-cult *key* to learn.
2. The *key* is the ability to be kind and respectful when feeling irritated, frustrated, or hurt.
3. Be angry and sin not. (Attitude)
4. Speak the truth in love. (Words)
5. Do all things through Christ. (Actions)
6. All things are possible to those who believe. (Trust)

Need and Weakness Cycle #2

Primary Need—Skeleton

A Skeleton's primary need in the area of curing present conflict is to feel listened to, empathized with, and learned from in every conflict situation. Skeletons want their feel-ings to be validated and understood by Skins. Skeletons aren't satisfied until Skins jump into Skeleton shoes and feel what they feel and think what they think. And the Skin has to learn from that situation—so the Skeleton doesn't get hurt in the future. Yes, empathy and understanding are oxygen for Skeletons. It is life to their souls—just like the air we breathe.

Primary Weakness—Skin

A Skin's primary weakness is receiving, supporting, and empathizing in the moment that they are feeling attacked by the Skeleton. The nature of the Skin is to be defensive. God designed skin to protect bones and organs. Therefore, when a Skin feels the frustration of a Skeleton, an internal switch flips on and a force field immediately surrounds that Skin. The force field defends the Skin from the Skeleton, and in so doing prevents the Skin from making that Skeleton feel better. What a deal! Right when the Skeleton needs humility, understanding, and empathy, the Skin, with a force field in place, can do nothing!

The bottom line in this situation is this: it doesn't take much to trigger that force field, and the Skeleton has a hard time not being abrasive. This deadly combination creates vicious cycle #2 in the area of Curing Present Conflict (CPC).

Summary

1. The Skeleton's primary need in the area of CPC is to feel listened to, empathized with, and learned from.
2. The Skin's primary weakness in the area of CPC is receiving, empathizing and learning in the moment that they feel attacked.

Curing Present Conflict: Main Skin Key

Skins can cope with Cycle #2 (CPC) when they have the character to listen, understand, and learn at the moment when they are feeling defensive. Sounds simple, but it's easier said than done, people. To be vulnerable and receiving when feeling defensive is almost too much to ask of Skins. When feeling attacked, every fiber of their being sounds the alarm. *Man the barricades! Up the force field!*

Key Scripture verses for the Skin are Matthew 5:25, 26 and Proverbs 15:1. In Matthew, Jesus urges us to "agree with our adversary quickly" before they take us for every penny. In Proverbs, Solomon teaches us that "a soft answer turns away wrath." If you are a dominant Skin in the relationship, by all means, commit these verses to memory and apply them to your life.

Defensives are to the Skeleton like blood is to a shark. In a scene in the children's movie, *Finding Nemo*, the sharks are having a support meeting for their addiction to eating fish. Their motto is *Fish are Friends, not Food*. They invite a couple of small fish to their meeting. During the meeting, when one of the fish starts bleeding, the main shark, Bruce, goes ballistic. Desperate for a meal of fish, he begins to hunt down the invited guests. The same thing usually happens when a Skin gets a defensive spirit and shows it. The Skeleton becomes a prosecuting attorney who will stop at nothing to prove that their issue is valid.

Listen up, Skins. Skeletons are into prevention. When you get defensive in a situation, it's a given that you are not into learning anything from that situation. Your understanding of a Skeleton's feelings and rationale for why they feel what they feel gives that Skeleton hope for a brighter future. Your humility makes the Skeleton feel that you are learning from the situation. If you are proud and non-receptive, the Skeleton loses hope and frustration builds. If you are receptive and humble, the Skeleton feels much better. Emotions are under control.

Being a "soft-throwing quarterback" is important for the Skeleton, but being a good wide receiver is a must for the Skin. If the Skin appears humble and vulnerable, with arms wide open, the Skeleton is less tempted to try to fire the ball in through the small hole. If the Skin appears to be receiving, humble, and able to understand even though feeling attacked, quarterbacks feel they can take something off their throw (soften it), and the ball will still be caught.

When the Skin gets defensive, the Skeleton is tempted to become a prosecuting attorney in an effort to prove the validity of their hurt and frustration. Even if the Skeleton has gone on the offensive, the Skin should do everything possible to avoid appearing defensive. Many times in scripture we read, *The humble will be exalted and the proud will be brought low*. Skins should have this verse ready as soon as Skeletons begin their critical tirades. The Skin that doesn't show immediate humility and understanding is asking for trouble.

Now, you might not agree with everything the Skeleton is saying, but you must believe that there is something true in what they are sharing. They are certainly right about how they feel, so at the very least you can understand their perspective—whether or not they are being what seems to be ridiculous and petty. Give the Skeleton humility and under-standing first, and then you will be able to get the under-standing that you need.

Empathy is a powerful resource that the Skin must learn to tap in to. Empathy is like soul food for Skeletons. It has an immediate calming effect. Being empathetic does not mean the Skin agrees with the Skeleton (*that is sympathetic*). Rather empathetic means that the Skin understands the Skeleton's perspective and feelings. The empathetic Skins puts on the Skeleton's shoes as it were, feels what the Skeleton is feeling, and convinces the Skeleton of that fact. The wise use of empa-thy will probably put a stop to the prosecution simply because there is no longer a defense attorney. Empathy is the "secret weapon" of the Skin, if they can develop that skill.

Summary

1. The number one character trait for the Skin to de-velop is the ability to listen, understand, and learn in the very moment they are feeling defensive.
2. Empathy is the most important key for the Skin to learn, and yet the most difficult.
3. The humble are exalted, but the proud are brought low.
4. You can do all things through Christ.
5. All things are possible to those who believe.

Of Surgeons and Chiropractors

The procedures patients endure in the offices and operating rooms of surgeons and chiropractors offer helpful parallels for the mindsets and attitudes we sometimes painfully endure in marriage. Let's begin in the OR (Operating Room).

When they wheel you on a gurney into the OR, it's a relief to know that the surgeon doesn't immediately start cutting on you. Before that happens, an anesthetist numbs the area that needs the work, or, if it's major, sends you to never-never land for awhile. Without anesthesia, there is no way a patient will allow the surgeon to work. And herein we find a useful lesson for Skeletons.

When conflict flares up, a Skeleton will often try to do surgery without anesthesia. Ouch! Hold on, Skeletons. Let's get some anesthesia into the picture before you try to straighten things out. You know? Anesthesia? Stuff like respect, appreciation, and encouragement—coming out of your mouth. If you want the Skin to listen to you, pump major amounts of anesthesia into them, and they just might hear what you have to say.

Now, looking at the Skins' side of things, we find that all they want is anesthesia and no surgery. Skins would just as soon sweep the problem under the carpet and let it go at that. They take a chance on non-surgery, and hope those trouble spots, whatever they are, will just go away. We know this happens from time to time, but for the most part, those old whatever-they-are's go from bad to worse. Avoiding surgery is not the answer. Skins, prosperity has a price tag. You need to pay it by going ahead with surgery even though conflict is uncomfortable—for everyone involved. Better to halt the cancer now! Before it spreads and becomes terminal. Go for the short-term pain. It will get you long-term gain.

Both Skins and Skeletons can learn from a trip to a

surgeon's operating room. It is a trip that benefits all marriages. Skeletons naturally focus on surgery and Skins focus on anesthesia. To be successful, the truth (surgery) must be spoken in love (anesthesia).

Now, let's take a trip to the chiropractor's office. You might not know this, but in addition to the chiropractor, you are most likely to find a massage therapist. These days you rarely find one without the other. The reason for this is that our bones and skin require separate treatments. Our bones need to be dealt with in one way, and our skin and muscles need to be dealt with in another way. On the bone side, the chiropractor needs to put pressure on exactly the right bone, or bones, to solve the problem. Skin has no desire for that kind of pressure. It would much rather be massaged by a talented therapist. Skin wants the soft rubbing while bones need pressure on the right spot, at the right time.

Do you see where this is going? Skeletons desire the right thing to be said, at the right time. (Puhlease, Skins! No manipulation. No maneuvering. We Skeletons hate it when Skins get round about or non-direct. No beating around the bush.) On the other hand, Skins don't usually go for the straight-ahead approach. Their preference is the soft, indirect, non-abrasive approach—tender, soothing words that communicate respect and loving affection. Skeletons want the truth directly, and the truth said right will set them free. Skins are less concerned with the truth itself than they are with the spirit (or environment) in which the truth is communicated. If the spirit isn't right, the truth isn't right to them. Skeletons prefer the verbal chiropractor. Skins prefer the verbal therapy.

Finding the Place of Agreement
(Q & A Session)

Question: Pastor Ken, I understand what you are saying about the keys to curing conflict, but what if I'm right?

Answer: Amen. I understand where you are coming from, but you know what? In a conflict the need to be right is what usually drives the conflict! None of us want to be wrong, nobody wants to lose. Why? Because of pride, good old-fashioned human pride. It's in the Bible. *Only by pride comes contention.* (Proverbs) There is no conflict if there is no pride, which there wouldn't be if we allow humility to step in and suggest, "I could be wrong." (*Hint, hint*)

Now, here is the second part of my answer: Would you rather be happy or right? For most people, deep down, the answer to this question is the former (happy). But sadly, most choose the latter most of the time. Yes, and it is tragic. We sacrifice relationships and everything that is good for us just to keep ourselves from appearing to be wrong. Everyone despises being wrong, even children. My own dear son, for example, used to cry profusely whenever I showed him that he was wrong about some issue—no matter how small. I ask you, why is it that we humans attach our personal value to whether or not we are right and perceived to be so?

Please understand. I am not saying that it is wrong to want to be right. It is human to want to be right. God created us that way. So be the human that God made you to be. For those of us who are believers, this means giving first place in our lives to the pursuit of His righteousness (Scripture?). And therein is a problem. There are two kinds of righteousness—His righteousness and self-righteousness (or my righteousness). Knowing which is which is hard oftentimes. His righteousness brings healing, liberation, and abundance. Self-righteousness is one of the most despicable of all sins. In short, it stinks. So, what am I getting at here? Simply this. Do not give up your desire to be right or to win, but at the same time be aware that doing so in the wrong way is hazardous to you, your spouse, and your marriage.

Despite the hazards, the payoff from a spirit of self-righteousness certainly can feel good. Yes, the sense of pride and the emotional high we get from feeling and acting like we are right fills us with a kind of drunken pleasure (self-righteousness wouldn't be a temptation if it didn't feel good). The bottom line, though, is that we've got to look at the long-term payoff. The fact is, the long-term payoff from our fight to be right is worthless. More than worthless, it is destructive. And sad to say, too many couples learn too late that broken relationships are not worth the rush that self-righteousness gives us in the short term.

Speaking as a Skeleton, I assure you that Skeletons are not right more often than Skins in CPC situations. The CPC keys do not favor one or the other. Rather, here is what favors both: a non-abrasive, non-defensive, humble attitude. With those we actually create an environment for what is needed most: a place of agreement in which both are right and both win. No, the Skeleton is not necessarily more right or wrong than the Skin. Both have strengths in quite different dimensions. Skeletons excel in discernment and effective strategizing (observation, planning, execution). For Skins, it is a whole different ballgame. For them, it is not what you do, but how you do it. Thus, their strength lies in acting in a right spirit—prudently, discreetly, and patiently. However, no matter how effectively each side uses their strengths, neither can claim to represent His righteousness perfectly. When all is said and done, it is God, not you, Who alone can rightly judge who is right and who is wrong.

In every situation, both are right and both are wrong in one way or another. Only God is completely right in every situation. You might be right with facts, but have a wrong spirit. You might have a right spirit, but have the facts wrong. What might be the right perspective for you to possess, could be the wrong perspective for the other person to have. My wife and I do our best to have the mindset that both are wrong and both are right. The spirit of self-righteousness will kill you, but submission to the righteousness of God will save you.

Both are right and both are wrong because we are human. This is the right way to think. This is the Spirit of Truth that will make you free. My wife and I have agreed that in every situation it is 50% her fault and 50% my fault, and that we will both give 120% to find a place of agreement. There is no way that one person is 100% right and the other 100% wrong. Trying to figure out percentages is a futile project. I want to recommend that you believe as my wife and I do in this area. We are both wrong, we are both right, we can both learn from the other, and we both have something to apologize for in every situation.

We have to constantly work hard to find a place of agreement.

My wife and I do not "agree to disagree." Many settle for this level of relationship... not me, not us. When people say to me, "Let's agree to disagree," I know that this person has some rebellion and self-righteousness in them. I know that they are committed to the satisfaction they get from feeling they are right in an area. I refuse to settle for a marriage where there is a spirit of disagreement. I believe that a win-win is possible in every situation. A win-win is a place of agreement, a place where both are right and both feel like they are winning. Valencia and I do whatever work it takes to reach this place in life, a place called peace and common ground. We have different hobbies, different styles, different, talents, different passions, and different personalities but we have worked to keep one mind and one spirit. Let's not settle for "Agreeing to Disagree." Let's do the work necessary to find and live in the place of agreement.

Question: Well, Pastor Ken, who's the Boss?

Answer: This is not the right question to dwell on. The spirit of the wife should be one of respect and trust in the leadership of her husband. The spirit of the wife should be one of a team-player, who respectfully shares her wisdom and strategies, but also has the spirit of trusting her husband to be the quarterback and make the right calls for the team. The husband should be constantly bouncing strategies off his wife and receiving her discernment and her wisdom. He should be taking a responsible spirit for the success of the home, feeling like the home rides on him. A thoughtful, humble spirit from the husband mixed with a respectful, team spirit from the wife is the recipe for success given in Ephesians 5. Husbands, love your wife. Wives, respect your Husbands.

Summary

1. Cut and separate. Ask and receive.
2. Punt if you need to.
3. Seal the deal. Both people sign.
4. Forgive quickly. Don't apologize too soon.

Speak for Yourself, The Other Appears

Speaking from my own experience in counseling married couples and borrowing from the wisdom of others, I've learned that when working things out the husband and wife should use "I" messages. What do I mean by this? Just this. *Talk for yourself, not the other person.*

For example, when explaining your heart and mind, say things like,

I felt hurt when _____ *was said.*

or

I felt angry and frustrated when _____ *happened.*

When you talk like this, no one can really argue with *you. After all, you did feel that way.* Sure, you may be wrong, but you still felt that way.

On the other hand, don't say,

You shouldn't have done _____.

or

You shouldn't have said _____.

When we speak like this, we make the assumption that we know about that other person. Assumptions rarely work and are usually hurtful. With that in mind, if and when we focus on the other person always use the words *seemed* or *appeared*.

For example, use phrasing such as,

You seemed to be meaning _____.

or

It appeared that you were saying _____.

By using the words *appear* or *seem* we are accomplishing a number of things. First, we avoid making assumptions. Secondly, we don't give place to the spirit of accusation and prosecution. Thirdly, the other person is given the benefit of the doubt. Most issues in marriage disagreements arise from misunderstandings. Things are rarely as they appear. We make things mean what they don't mean on most occasions just because our brains think differently.

Using the word *appear* and *seem* will save us much time, pain, and suffering. Yes, it's a humble word, but humility always turns into victory.

Make it Big, Make it Small

For Skeletons, being kind and respectful when feeling irritated, frustrated, or hurt is easier said than done. Being humble and receiving when feeling attacked is equally hard for Skins.

If responding positively when feeling negatively were easy, there wouldn't be a 50% divorce rate. I would not be writing this book. The fact is that most couples are not willing to pay the price to go down the narrow path. If you have the will and passion to create some heaven on earth, I have a few practical ideas for you.

When sharing feelings of irritation, frustration, or hurt with Skins, Skeletons are likely to make a big deal about it. They like to use fancy nouns, huge adjectives and explosive verbs. And they do so in a passionate tone of voice. Their assumption is that by painting a really dramatic, emphatic picture, Skins will receive it with greater intensity and be all the more empathetic. In reality, the opposite happens. In making a big deal about the situation, Skeletons make Skins feel more disrespected, and thus more likely to go on the defensive.

I have found that my dear Skin receives it so much better when I make my issue and hurt small instead of gigantic. So, I try to say things that soften the blow. Things such as,

Hey, honey, this is no big deal, and I realize I'm in a sensitive mood etc., etc.

or

I'm super thankful for all your hard work, and I know you didn't mean to do anything, etc. etc.

Speaking like this, I am usually much more successful.

By "making it little," I don't trigger the natural defensive tendency of my Skin.

To borrow another analogy from football, don't throw the ball as hard to a child as you would to an adult. Take something off the throw, Skeleton. Do it whenever it appears that your Skin has caused you to feel irritation, frustration, or hurt.

On the other hand, Skins should make a huge deal about the Skeleton's issue. This is not always a simple matter because Skins tend to minimize things. As in the following:

I can't believe he/she is making such a big deal out of this ... This is the dumbest, most ridiculous problem I've ever heard of ...

or

My spouse needs to get a life.

To a Skeleton, minimizing the importance of an issue sounds like defense, like the Skin is trying to skirt the issue and sweep it under the carpet. This invalidates the Skeleton's hurt and frustration and tempts the Skeleton to make the issue bigger and bigger. When this happens (and it happens often), a mini-cycle develops within the big cycle, and suddenly the conflict is more intense than ever.

To avoid this, Skins need to make a huge deal about a Skeleton's issues. When they do, Skeletons feel like they don't have to "make it big." So Skins, bring to bear the full force of your language skills—big, emphatic nouns; colorful adjectives; lively verbs. Spoken in an earnest, sincere tone of voice, these really help Skeletons tone down and get a better perspective.

Don't Teach the Lesson! Learn It!

When Skeletons experience irritation, frustration, or hurt, they have an overriding desire to prevent it from ever happening again. This is their hope for a brighter tomorrow. Importantly, it helps them to forgive and move on. For their part, Skins want Skeletons to do just that. *Take a chill pill,* you might hear a Skin telling his/her partner, *and stop getting so bent out of shape over every little deal. Just let's end the conflict as quickly as possible and move on with life.*

"Less is More" is an effective watchword for Skeletons trying to teach Skins the lesson from situations, but, to the surprise of Skeletons, Skins don't care about the lesson, much less learn it. First and foremost, they are interested in defense, in getting the problem over with as quickly as possible. That done, they can start feeling liked and respected again.

Every once in a while, a small amount of lesson teaching is okay, but most of the time Skeletons should leave the teaching and growth to God. In my case, I know that He does a much better job on Valencia than I could ever hope to do. I recognize that she appreciates my involvement in her growth process and I receive that as part of my purpose, but when all is said and done, "Less is More."

Continuing on this theme, let me add that no two situations are alike. I could teach my wife what the right thing to do is in one situation, but in the future there will probably not be one that is exactly like it. So, what my wife really needs is a better sense of discernment—not the legalistic, exact lesson that can be learned from that single situation. Discernment cannot be learned from legalistically analyzing and tearing apart the situation. The Skin can probably do that without your help, and get more out of doing it than by you trying to teach them.

Trying to cram the lesson down the Skin's throat doesn't really work unless you do it in a perfectly God-like manner. Have you ever wondered why, after ten years, your spouse still does things that you have been teaching them not to do? It's because they have not heard one of your lessons. There is a difference between "hearing" and hearing. That is why Jesus said, "To him who has ears to hear let him hear." Jesus realized that very few who heard Him would actually "hear" Him. The same is true with your spouse. If they are feeling defensive at all they will not "hear" you; they will merely humor you just enough to get the problem over with. So, leave the lesson-giving mostly to God, and you will be better off.

Doing that effectively requires that we Skeletons truly learn the meaning of the simple word "trust." Skeletons are horrible at trusting the Skin and at trusting God. "Let Go and Let God" is a great motto for any Skeleton to have. (It should be noted that this is not a great motto for a Skin—they are already too good at that.) Teaching the Lesson is a defense mechanism of the Skeleton. They figure that the only way to avoid being hurt or frustrated again is by changing the Skin. Yet, by trying to change the Skin instead of letting God do the bulk of it, the Skeleton's lessons tend to drown out the voice of God. So, *trust in the Lord and He will give you the desires of your heart.*

The Skin, on the other hand, should really try to learn the lesson from each situation. Evaluated experience is the greatest teacher. The Skin should seek to understand the situation, why it happened, and how each person could have handled it better. The Skin should give hope to the Skeleton by making the Skeleton think that there is a chance that this problem won't happen again. The Skeleton will only have hope for a better life when they feel that the Skin has really understood and learned. When the Skeleton feels that the Skin has really learned the lesson, forgiveness is easy because the Skeleton has hope.

The challenge is for the Skin to relay this "lesson learned" impression to the Skeleton so that the Skeleton truly believes that there is a chance that life could get better. It is very hard for the Skin to communicate this lesson-learned mentality to the Skeleton because they are probably feeling defensive. Once again, the Skin needs to focus on losing the defensive spirit. The defensive spirit does not allow for lessons learned. Lessons are only learned with a humble spirit. Be strong and clear when giving the "lesson learned" message to the Skeleton. Let the Skeleton know you understand what happened, why it happened, and why there is a chance it won't happen again. Say it with passion and make sure the Skeleton gets your point.

When the Skeleton feels that you have learned what can be learned, the Skeleton will feel loved and hence very forgiving. It will really soften the spirit, and fill the need of Skeletons. It really helps them to drop it and let it go. When it appears that you are sweeping it under the carpet, the Skeleton feels like they need to keep driving it home. Assure your Skeleton that you are humble and have learned, and you will enjoy the fruit.

Be Sincere, Be Fair

Skins need to be sincere—something that is easier said than done. They tend to bounce back and forth from defending to avoiding by faking a win. In other words, they will play the martyr just to get the conflict over with. They will act like everything is all right just to get done. They will pretend to get a win, but in actuality they took a loss and they know it.

The problem with this tendency is that the Skeleton thinks that the Skin ended up happy, and feels very deceived when He/she finds out in the end that the Skin wasn't happy after all. Thus, because Skins have a tendency to play the martyr by faking apologies and happiness, sincerity is extremely important.

If the Skin plays the martyr in a conflict just to get it over and done with, it really isn't over, is it? No, this issue will show up again. But the next time it is brought up, it will be during another issue and it may take much more time and effort to finally resolve that problem. It is best to solve and resolve each conflict completely and entirely as they arise.

Skins, do not fake agreement when you do not have agreement in your heart. Do the work that it takes to find that place of agreement. You might have to be creative, but you can find agreement in every situation. Be sincere and authentic because deception will always come back to bite the both of you.

The Skeleton needs to make sure that He/she is being fair, and needs to make sure that the Skin feels like every issue ends up with a fair, win-win agreement. Skeletons can get so consumed with their own win that they forget to make sure that the Skin also gets a win. So, make sure that your Skin gets a win in every situation. If your Skin gets a loss, then you also get a loss, and a very big loss in the end. Ask the Skin on a regular basis if they feel better. I frequently ask my wife questions like, "Are you sure that you feel better?" and "Are you sure you got a win in this situation?" or "Is there anything else that I need to make right with you?" Don't completely trust the Skin to get their own win, make sure they are happy at the end of the conflict.

Skins naturally feel like Skeletons are unfair. Skeletons do, for the most part, really want to be fair, but fail to make sure that they are in the mind of the Skin. Ask the Lord to help you be fair in every situation. He will help you.

Character Branding, Reasons for Doing

Skeletons must avoid branding the Skin with verbiage that makes Skins feel like they are being branded with disrespect. Remember that the number one need of the Skin in curing conflict is to feel liked and respected. All it takes is one wrong word to brand the Skin with disrespect.

There are certain words that I know are off-limits in conversations because they will, in my wife's mind, brand her. These words are pitfalls that the Skeleton should make note of as time goes and avoid them at all cost.

Here is an example of what I am talking about. Valencia works much harder than me physically, and puts high value on hard, physical work (something she acquired from her dad). If anyone tends to be lazy, it's me. I battle the couch potato syndrome constantly, and, to make matters worse, I despise working out (not a good thing when you have my metabolism.) Well, every once in a while I feel like my wife didn't think something through concerning me like I thought she should, so out of my mouth comes something accusatory like, "Quit being lazy-brained." Now, in saying that I don't mean to say that she is a lazy person, but I have learned that the word "lazy" triggers a kind of character assassination in her. The word just plain shuts her down because she feels branded with a disrespected character quality. After doing it a few times, I learned to phrase things much more graciously: "Honey, could you please think things through a bit more before you ..."

Another problem for Skeletons is their continual use of the words *always* and *never*. Skins use them too, but Skeletons spit them out like so many sunflower seeds at a ball game. "You *never* change." "You *always* forget to buy the right thing," Again, when Skins hear these kinds of remarks, it feels like character assassination. In addition to being accused of committing one small, wrong act, they feel labeled as complete losers. Skeleton, this ought not to be. Learn to separate the person from the deed. Make sure that you protect and respect your Skin and let them know that you don't think this is who the person is. Here is a much better way of putting things: "You are doing so much better in this area, but this action hurt my feelings." So remember: always stay away from *never* and never say *always*.

Because Skins are naturally defensive, they love to give what seems to them to be logical reasons for doing what they do or not doing what they should have done. They will say something like, "The reason I didn't do that was ..." or "The reason I did that was because you did this." Skin, don't use any reasons to justify your actions or intentions. To a Skeleton they just sound like huge excuses and a lack of responsibility for your part in the problem. Again, skeletons hate reasons. They want Skins to take responsibility for whatever they did, to learn from it, and to apologize for it eventually. Reasons will ruin all of that in a Skeleton's mind. Reasons will just make matters worse. In the Skeleton's mind there is never a good reason to hurt them. Skins, make sure that you separate what you meant to do from what you did do. Take responsibility for your actions no matter how sincere or right your intentions may have been. In other words, do not give reasons for why you did what you did.

Protect Intentions, Actions Speak

For Skins, intentions are who they are. When they give reasons explaining why they did what they did, their motive is to protect their intentions. When they think their intentions are being questioned, they feel like they are being branded with disrespect and dislike. So, Skeletons, work hard at not disrespecting the intentions of your Skin. When "accusing" your Skin of something, separate the intention from the action. Skeletons tend to blow things out of proportion, and Skins rarely mean any harm by what they do. So a Skeleton should say something like, "I know you didn't mean it, but you accidentally hurt my feelings." Putting it that way goes a long way towards protecting a Skin's feelings.

Bottom line, Skin, actions speak much louder than words.

Your Skeleton doesn't care what you *mean* to do. The fact is you didn't mean to do the right thing to them in the first place. That is why their feelings are hurt. The cause of the Skeleton's hurt is your under-thinking, and if you use it as an excuse, you are protecting your intentions *and* deepening your Skeleton's hurt. Skins, you can protect your intentions and take full responsibility for your actions by saying something like this: "I know what I did to you was completely wrong, and you hate it when I under-think. I just want you to know I didn't mean it the way that it appeared."

Just as Skeletons should separate the intentions and actions of Skins, Skins should do likewise. This takes what I call "separation conversation" between the two. Separation conversation is important, fair, and a win-win. It's just like a child saying, "One for me, one for you." Or, as in a card game when you deal a card to the other player and then one to yourself. You don't deal seven cards to yourself and then seven to the other person. So also, your mindset in separation conversation should be as follows: both the Skin and the Skeleton separate actions from intentions, taking full responsibility for actions, while at the same time protecting the motives, heart, and intentions of the other.

Timeouts

Spokane, Washington is home to Gonzaga University, a small college with a big bite. Most years, its tenacious men's basketball team—the Bulldogs—are somewhere in the middle of the NCAA Division I Top Twenty-five. Quite an honor for a school of its size, but the recognition is well earned. The 'Dogs usually play a schedule with games resembling the match-up between David and Goliath, with David being you-know-who.

In some of these battles, the lead seesaws back and forth right down to the end. Usually, both coaches are forced to use most, if not all, of their team's allotment of time outs. Calling time out usually occurs when the opponent has gained the upper hand. Huddling with his players at the sideline, he outlines a play, offers some encouragement, and perhaps makes a substitution or two. These moves have one purpose—to shift the momentum back in his direction. And very often, when play resumes, that is exactly what happens.

Yes, time outs really can make a difference—in basketball, and in resolving marital conflicts. When a Skeleton is getting more and more disrespectful, when a Skin is becoming more and more defensive, when the tide of stubbornness and intensity is rising fast, please, somebody call time out! And not just a thirty-second time out. Make it a full!

In time out, it is up to both persons to acknowledge the vicious cycle, and to accept personal responsibility for turning it around. And this they can do with words such as these:

> **Skin:** *"I will receive what you are saying if you will please just make it more user-friendly."*

> **Skeleton:** *"I will be happy to start treating you with respect, if you will receive what I am saying."*

Time outs are genuine opportunities for couples to strategize for change. When done properly and fairly, they really can turn conflicts around.

Kicking It Away

In football, when a team reaches fourth down and is out of field goal range, the coach has to make a decision. He can "go for it" (put the ball into play in hopes of gaining the yards necessary for a first down), or he can punt (kick the ball to the other team, in hopes of getting it back in couple of minutes or so).

Now, I want to be very careful on this point, because someone could use what I am about to say as an excuse to do the wrong thing. When a conflict resolution is going in the wrong direction and showing no signs of improvement, the best thing to do is punt. Punting gives you a short break. There's time to cool down, regain poise, and rethink the game plan. If "play resumes" and things still don't go well, well, just punt again and go through the process again. Give yourself a break, cool down, regain poise, etc., etc. Do whatever it takes, and as often as it takes.

Okay, now, I need to lay down a few ground rules about punting. Remember, when a team punts, it doesn't mean that the team is no longer in the game mentally. No one should become passive aggressive.

Plus, the *way* that you punt is extremely important. Both people must be okay with the punt. Punt rudely, and the problem will only be worse when you come back. Going to another room is fine, but don't leave the premises. Walking out of the house, getting into the car, and driving off should never happen. Do that, especially with a bad spirit, and you are practicing divorce.

While apart, both persons should focus on getting a right

spirit. Skeletons need to lose their abrasive spirit and replace it with respect and kindness. Skins need to shed their defensive spirit and put on humility and understanding. After a few minutes, with the adjustments made, one or the other should try to get the conversation going again.

With both back and talking again, things still may not be any better. This will occur if one or both did get not their spirit right while out the first time. In that case, you probably need to line up for another punt formation. Make sure your punt is a good one this time. Sometimes one of the persons did not get their spirit right because the punting by the other person was rude. To avoid rudeness when you punt, try something like this on for size:

Honey, I am being abrasive and you are on the defensive. Would it be okay if we took a small break just to get our spirits right, so this conversation will work?"

When you put it that way, you can be pretty sure that the other person will agree to the punt. But don't give them a "Mary Kay facial" on your way out of the room. Do that and the punt will be worthless

Forgive Quickly, Don't Apologize Too Soon

Skeletons have a very hard time forgiving and letting go. We covered this briefly in *Don't Teach the Lesson, Learn It.* Skeletons are so worried about preventing the next problem down the road that forgiveness does not come easily. They don't just want this problem over with, they want to prevent the next one. Because of their desire to prevent, they are consumed with the sincerity and integrity of the Skin, as well as learning the lesson that should be learned. Forgiveness is easy, but not before these heart needs have been fulfilled: understanding, sincere listening, and proper apologies. This is especially true if the Skin is defensive in the situation. The Skin will say some things that are not entirely true. The same is true when the Skeleton is being abrasive; their presentation of the problem is exaggerated. When the Skin makes an extreme comment, the Skeleton, being a great counter of outrageous statements, will make a mental note of it. Later, during the course of a growth opportunity (conflict) the Skeleton may blurt out three or four of the outrageous comments the Skin had blurted out earlier. The Skeleton will want the Skin to individually reverse the logic of all these comments. To the Skeleton these strongholds of thought must be torn down because they will most likely lead to future problems. Therefore, Skin, it is your duty to take back every wrong thought pattern before the Skeleton is willing to forgive.

My advice to the Skeleton is to forgive as quickly as possible. Pick your battles carefully, and every once in a while just forgive. Forgiving when the Skin doesn't deserve it is a great way to create positive momentum and/or reverse negative momentum.

Skins love a forgiving spirit. When you put on a forgiving spirit, Skeleton, you are telling your Skin that He/she is liked and respected. They want to feel like you can't wait to forgive them. They want to feel like you respect them so much, and appreciate them so much, that forgiveness is easy. They think that because they did something for you earlier in the day, something that you remember and causes you to cut them some major slack on some little thing that they didn't do. So, Skeletons, every once in a while, just forgive without it having to be earned.

Skins, on the other hand, need to be careful not to apologize too soon. Skeletons consider an apology made too soon to be like trying to have an orgasm without foreplay. I don't mean to be graphic or gross, but conflict resolution for a Skeleton is more about the foreplay than the orgasm. When the Skin apologizes before the understanding and the learning, the Skeleton feels like the Skin is just trying to sweep things under the carpet. When the apology is made too soon, the Skeleton chalks it up as insincere. The more apologies the Skin makes that don't work, the harder and harder it gets to convince the Skeleton that the sorrow is genuine. As the Skin's apologies pile up, the Skeleton becomes more and more skeptical and growth in the marriage grinds to a halt. So to avoid the appearance of insincerity, Skins, listen and understand first, then apologize.

Section 3

Prevention

Prevention

Moving Into Level Four

Here we are—at the fourth-level marriage. This is the level where both of you have made the proper adjustments, where the chemistry is working just right. Reaching this level takes time, mucho effort, killing the flesh, and massive personal growth on both sides. But it is worth it! Your relationship can be (no kidding) heaven-on-earth!

Now, up front, I am sorry to have to inform you that only a very small percentage of marriages reach this point. But, hey, take heart. If your marriage reaches level three, you are already in the minority! So just by reaching level four, it is certain that the two of you have already found a great deal of happiness and fulfillment.

Now, as we move into this level, realize that conflict is not going to disappear once and for all. This level is about preventing *some* conflict, not all of it. Make no bones about it, as long as you are human, and as long as you live on this planet, conflict and the potential for conflict are always going to be there. Rather than spend time wishing it weren't here, let's learn how to deal with it.

Need and Weakness Cycle #1

As partners in a marital relationship, we have to continually remind ourselves that the relationship is shared. When a Skin and Skeleton declare those vows, they form a relationship in which each one makes a unique contribution in completing one another and in preventing cycles of conflict.

As we have seen, these cycles arise out of the needs and weaknesses of both partners. Probably the greatest need of Skins is being accepted and respected the way they are. Yes, warts and all! There is still room for growth and maturity in many areas.

As for Skeletons, their greatest weakness lies in choosing to go to war over every negative situation that comes up, to solve every problem by "fixing" the Skins.

We can well see that conflict is bound to arise when things go wrong. Let's have a look at how to prevent it.

Main Skeleton Key: Chill!

From one Skeleton to another, let me tell it like it is. In general, we are waaayyyy too uptight about little issues. Waaaaayyyyyy too stressed out. The answer for us is, in short, this: CHILL!

Chilling involves a number of things, but first off, know

that "chill" is an attitude. Start with this—relax. You do this by learning to stop sweating the small stuff. Let some things go. Stop waging warfare on a massive front where, let's face it, the odds are stacked against you. Instead, choose your battles. And try this one for size—develop some *unawareness*. Yes, *un*awareness, i.e. not noticing every little thing. Finally, how about this. Resign from being General Manager of the Universe. Leave that position to God. Indeed, as it has oft been said, *Let go and let God!*

In simple terms, chilling is an attitude, a "spirit thing." It comes on like a front of balmy weather—mild, pleasant, peaceful. As an attitude, it exudes patience, trust, and joy.

Skins want to be left alone. They don't want to feel picked on. As for us Skeletons, we have way too many irritations. So, we have got to let God develop in us an attitude of relaxation and laughter—a great big "It's no big deal." If we don't learn this spirit, evolving as a person becomes impossible. Without a thicker skin towards hurts and irritations (the result of a crucified fleshly nature), life will not be enjoyable and neither will our marriage. I make no bones about it, a spirit of Chill is the most important Skeleton key for success on marriage level 4.

Need and Weakness Cycle # Two

Skeleton Need: Thoughtfulness, Awareness, and Discernment

Skin Weakness: Being Oblivious, Unaware, and Undiscerning

Do you see the potential for a problem here? The Skeleton's number one love language need is thoughtfulness, awareness, discernment, and timing from the Skin. These things are hard to get from Skins because they tend to have tunnel vision and are unaware many times of what is going on around them. When they feel pressured or nervous, the problem gets twice as bad. So, timing is not the strength of the Skin, and once again we have a situation where the need of one is paired together with the weakness of the other. I think we all need to have a talk with Adam when we get to heaven. I don't think he understands all that he has put us through. May God bless as you Skins become more alert and discerning and you Skeletons learn to be forgiving and chilled out.

Main Skin Key: Read Their Mind!

The title of this section comes from a statement that is commonly used by many defensive-minded people: *You can't expect me to read your mind!*

What a classic Skin statement! And here's why. Skins prefer to be asked, in a nice way, to do something rather than think of it on their own.

Reading someone's mind seems like an impossible task, and, of course, I'm being a little dramatic (for effect) on this one. Yet there is something true to life about this statement. *Read my mind.* When a Skin reads the mind of their spouse, their spouse will feel loved—to the bone!

Let's break this concept down a little more. The Skeleton's #1 need in the area of prevention is for the Skin to be thoughtful, tuned into, and aware. In other words, to be up-to-date about the subject matter whirling around in their Skeleton's cognitive processes (aka brain waves). To do this, Skins have to develop a good radar system. They have to be aware of their partner's basic brain "drift." As this happens, Skeletons feel very tuned into their Skins. They are aware of what their Skin is up to, and feel loved when the same actions are returned to them. The Skin's #1 weakness is their tendency to be oblivious of what is going on in the skeletal mind. This lack of awareness can be hurtful.

When Skeletons feel studied and meditated on, they feel loved. Speaking out of my relationship with Valencia, I feel loved when she:

▸ Is aware of what is in my mind.
▸ Is tuned into my emotions and acts in accordance with them.
▸ Understands my irritations, and is careful not to add to them.
▸ Is aware of my plans, and is careful not to mess them up.
▸ Checks with me before making important decisions.
▸ Buys my favorite soda from the store, or makes my favorite dish for dinner.
▸ Hugs me when I want to be hugged and stays away from me when I want to be left alone to focus.
▸ Knows what I'm feeling, what I'm wanting, and what I'm thinking.

No question about it, Valencia deserves a lot of credit for

taking time and energy, over a number of years, to study me, to figure me out. The result is that she reads me pretty well. *Most* of the time, her intuition is right on. And the rest of the time? Well, we both know that her intuition is off at just about the time when my "Chill Spirit" isn't what it should be either (oh well, what else is new?).

So, the process goes on. Valencia continues to learn to tune into me. Knowing how my brain works, she can usually discern when to do what and when not to do what, etc. Thanks to her, I feel very loved. The bottom line is that she is doing just a fabulous job of developing intuition, reading my mind, and speaking what experts call my "love language."

Trust, Wait

Trust is *the* key word for Skeletons. Trust the Lord a bit more, trust your spouse a bit more, and trust your kids a bit more. Trust God to change your spouse. Don't do your job *and* God's job.

A Skeleton tends to think that He/she is called to be the CEO of the universe. Hey, skell, give yourself a break! Taking on that position will leave you bone-weary as all get out. And it'll stay that way until you start focusing on challenges relative to you and avoiding those that aren't.

Worry and over-thinking are pandemic among Skeletons. So, therefore, it behooveth them to believe to the marrow of their bones that everything is going to be fine; God is in the control tower. What I am about to say is hard to believe, but I'll say it anyway. If you dropped off the planet for some horrible reason, your spouse and your kids would make it without you. The world would keep spinning. This may seem impossible to you, Skeletons. But not when you resign from the position of CEO of the Universe, and let God execute a friendly corporate takeover. Skeletons, let go and let God!

For Skins, the key word is *wait*. And here is why. Skins have a problem with under-thinking. They tend not to think before they act. They make assumptions to save time, and their assumptions usually end up wrong-headed and off base.

By waiting, a Skin takes the time to carefully think things through, to ponder, for example, what to say or do in any given situation. Acting before thinking is deeply repugnant to Skeletons, so by cultivating a habit of waiting, Skins inject a positive new spirit of carefulness into the marital chemistry.

Jesus once told his followers, *My sheep know my voice* (John 10:27). By waiting, Skins give themselves time for the Holy Spirit to take control of situations. Over the years, through diligent, careful practice, Valencia has become very adept at listening for and heeding the Spirit's checks, reminders, and counsel. For example, just as she is about to act on a wrong assumption about me, the Holy Spirit will put a little check, or restraint, into her mind and spirit. Just as a hockey player gets "checked off" the puck by a defender, so Valencia is checked off her course of action. The process works extremely well. That little check by the Lord helps her to slow down and make the right decision.

Ready, Aim; Ready, Fire

This section is cousin to *Trust, Wait,* but it stands well on its own.

Picture someone discharging a pistol. Picture a firearms coach telling a student, "Ready, aim, fire!" This is similar to the three-step sequence used by track officials to start races: "On your mark ... get set ... go!" Let's look at these sequences for a moment to see how they apply in level-four relationships.

Holding Their Fire ...

When a Skeleton makes decisions and choices, his/ her tendency is to be a shooter that goes like this: ready, aim, aim, aim, aim, aim, aim and then (*maybe*) fire (*if everything is just right*)! Why? Well, here's the deal. Skeletons usually have a bad case of paralysis of analysis. They *over-think* everything. And because of this tendency, they can't understand why, by nature, Skins *under-think* everything. Skeletons, you need to think a little less and be more decisive for the sake of yourself, your spouse, and your marriage.

Asking Questions Later ...

Because under-thinking is a major tendency and weakness of Skins, it follows that they don't think enough before taking action. Their predisposition is "ready, fire!" (*no aiming*). Okay, fine, it is just a tendency, not true in every situation. But, because it is true most of the time, Skins make a lot of mistakes in their often-misguided efforts to love their over-thinking spouses. Working harder, not smarter, they end up cleaning up a lot of situations—something which, as you might guess, does not go down well with Skeletons. Skeletons want to be the object of carefully considered actions, not experimentation. Without significant reprogramming, however, Skins will continue to act and hope for the best while Skeletons think, think, and think, without leaving room for action.

Meaning, Appearance of Evil

Crunching the Numbers

Skeletons do way too much math. Their motto is *Actions speak way louder than words*. Using overactive mental calculators, they determine the intentions of Skins based on their perception of action and inaction. When all the numbers are in and added up, they feel sure that their data equals a certain meaning.

The problem with doing this is that their Skin usually meant nothing by what they did or did not do. In fact, the Skin was probably not even thinking or intending anything by what they did or did not do. Ironically, their problem is not cruel intentions, but simply under-thinking. Living life on cruise control is what Skins love to do, so assuming that a Skin planned on doing what they did is usually a mistake.

Things are what they are. We Skeletons add way too much meaning to situations. We have got to stop the major drama. We make mountains out of molehills, because, in so many situations, we bring all sorts of meaning that wasn't there until we added it. What Skins do doesn't mean that they don't love you, that they don't care about you, or that they are selfish and stubborn. Well, okay, some of that might be true at times, but usually they are simply oblivious. So, remember, Skeletons: things are usually not what they appear to be.

Steering Clear of ...

Skins, on the other hand, should remember the scripture verse: *Abstain from all appearance of evil* (1 Thessalonians 5:22). They should remember that Skeletons are extremely aware of how you do what you do. They read body language, monitor tones of voice, measure intensity, note the time it takes you to act, etc. They not only gather all of this data, but they also create meaning and language out of your every appearance. And, typically, the meaning they create is negative. So, be very careful. Make sure that you are careful about your body language, facial expressions, voice tones, and time lapse (the time it takes you to do something).

Here are a couple of examples of how I typically tend to add meaning to Val's every action and non-action:

If she hurts my feelings and I know that she knows and it takes her an hour to call to help me feel better, I don't feel cared for. I don't feel cared for because I calculated the amount of her concern for me according to my watch. If she had called me after ten minutes instead of an hour, I would've felt much more loved.

If Val leans in to kiss me, I feel more loved than if I lean in to kiss her and she just waits for my kiss.

Thank God for her. In learning to avoid the appearance of evil, she is aware of her body language and the message it is sending me.

Ask Nicely, Do Before Asked

Skeletons in the School of Asking

As we discussed earlier in this Section, Skeletons feel love at its best when their Skin-mates read their minds and act accordingly. This sounds cool, but here's what often happens. Skeletons prefer to simply expect their needs to be met rather than asking nicely. They bounce back and forth from the extreme of never asking to the extreme of asking with irritation and disrespect. This mindset is as unhealthy and unworkable as it sounds. And here is the way out, Skeletons. Stop believing that you won't, or don't, feel love when you have to ask. Instead, realize that in order for reaping to take place, you have to do some sowing. Try this, for example. Learn to ask nicely twenty times without expecting to receive one thoughtful act in return. Then, when your Skin-mate reads your mind and does something that's totally "right," you will flood her/him with heartfelt thankfulness. Plus, you will definitely see the value of learning (*forcing yourself to do so if necessary*) to ask nicely for your needs to be met.

I was talking about this subject the other day with a Skeleton gentleman in my church. He gave me an illustration that I have his permission to share.

In terms that made my mouth water, the gentleman told me that his favorite dinner dish is beef, and that chicken is a distant second. Having informed his wife of his love for beef a time or two, he assumes that his wife firmly grasps the fact, and is well aware of how much it means to him. Now, this gentleman's wife is an incredible individual and a typical, easy-going Skin. However, she enjoys chicken more than beef, and is probably convinced that it is healthier than cow. So, naturally, instead of choosing steak or roast beef for dinner, she gravitates towards good old fried chicken or chicken potpie. And it's not because she doesn't love her husband. It's just that, being Skin natured, she is easy-going and running on cruise control.

Now, notice the husband's response. He explained to me that, rather than asking for beef more often, he eats mostly chicken and gives his wife her way. Why? Because, as he told me, if he asks for beef, and gets it, he doesn't feel loved. (Yes, being true to his Skeleton nature, he'd rather not get, than ask.)

Well, speaking as a Skeleton to Skeletons, here is what I recommend for this situation. Aim at putting the Skin—in this case the wife—in a win/win situation, one in which he gets his beef and she gets her chicken. He could do this by, for example, giving his wife some money and asking her to go out and buy some steak for dinner. (Not a bad way to ask nicely, right?) Now, I would forewarn the gentleman that he probably might not feel loved right away. So, he might try a second and third time, if necessary. And then he should get ready. Down the road, those feelings will rise and spill over when she, with a smile on her face, surprises him with one of the most delicious steak dinners ever.

Now, having offered some of my best, most considered advice, I realize what our typical Skeletal response to this idea of asking nicely often is: *My Skin should care about me enough to know!*

How often have I heard these angry, frustrated words come whining out of my own mouth! How unloved, uncared for, and angry have we Skeletons felt every time we have had to ask in order to get our needs met! Why, even the mention of having to do it is cause for anger!

Well, there is really no alternative, fellow Skeletons. Asking nicely is what we have to do to receive those feelings of love down the road. And I say this knowing full well that asking nicely is obviously not something we were born with. In reality, it is a learned skill, acquired by training.

So, go ahead. Ask freely. And freely you shall receive. Ask nicely. And the feelings of love will be there eventually, and in God's good time.

Skins Behaving Proactively

Now, speaking to Skins, here's how to have a happy Skeleton spouse (no small job, to be sure). Learn to do the right thing, buy the right thing (their kind of soda, for example), and say the right thing *before* being asked. Remember what they say, remember the words they like, remember the kinds of gifts they like. And in all of this, take notes. Take notes of your Skeleton's wants, timings, and desires. And, oh, yes, above all, remember to tune into your Skeleton's love language (i.e. read his/her mind!)

The above job description pretty well boils down to one thing—being *proactive*. The proactive Skin acts before being asked but not by guesswork or assumptions. Proactive action involves asking your Skeleton what is wanted and when.

Realize that Skeletons appreciate being asked in the right situations, but don't forget—they hate being the one doing the asking. When a Skin stays one step ahead of a Skeleton's requests, that Skin will be successful. Call before they call you, do the job before they mention it, say something about it before they say something, and buy it before they ask for it. Follow after these things, and, behold, there shall be peace, love, and joy in thy home.

But let's face it, Skins. Doing all that stuff is hard. For

you, pro-activity is a huge job, one that "don't come easy." There are reasons for this. For one thing, you tend to bounce back and forth between dependence (*just ask me, hon*) and independence (*so leave me alone, okay?*). Another reason is that it really bugs you to have to be thinking about and discerning all of your Skeleton's little needs, thoughts, and desires. Don't be like the many Skins who spend sixteen hours a day on the job with the excuse that they are "providing" for their Skeletons. That kind of gross misappropriation of time and energy explains why so many guys (and gals) who burn so much time at work to buy gadgets and baubles for their spouse end up seeing them walk out of the marriage unloved, used up, and empty. It's sad, and unnecessary.

So, remember, Skins. Skeletons would rather be thought of than worked for. Of course, that does not mean that Skeletons should not show a lot of appreciation for the long, hard hours that Skins put in. They should and they must. But never forget that, in the heart and mind of a Skeleton, blood, sweat, and tears at the workplace cannot replace thoughtfulness and intuition.

Write it Down, Bring it Up

Households are corporations. Successful corporations cannot function without regular staff meetings, yet we try to run quality homes without them.

Husbands and wives should see themselves as presidents and vice-presidents. Each couple should have a weekly staff meeting to discuss issues and make plans. With weekly meetings and a written agenda, you will feel secure and assured, knowing that issues will be addressed, plans drawn up, and action taken.

Taking Notes

Skeletons need all the help they can get managing their frustrations. Something that helps a lot is writing them down for discussion at staff meeting. Putting them on paper gives Skeletons relief from the pressure for the time being.

Skeletons like to manage problems as they go. This creates more problems. For one thing, managing every little problem on the fly triggers a defensive mechanism in Skins. They regard Skeletons as nags—always sweating the small stuff. Avoid this by making a list of your issues and taking care of them later at the meeting. This will hold your emotions in check in the meantime, and reduce the number and complexity of your problems. Voila! A more peaceful, happier home is created.

Getting After It (In a Nice Way)

Skin, by all means, don't waste time waiting to bring up issues. Get your Skeleton (nicely), before He/she gets you (in the wrong way). Be proactive; it's your most effective defense. If you get the slightest inkling that there could be tension in a situation, bring it up immediately. Ask your Skeleton questions such as, "Did I hurt your feelings?" or "Did I bother you?" And make sure you say things sincerely. If you do it right, you will be putting out the fire before it really gets started.

Pro-activity would be more common among Skins except that they have this weakness that holds them back. It is this: when a Skin feels that something is wrong with their Skeleton, they tend to hope their senses are wrong. They figure, "Why make an issue out of something if it's not there. If there is an issue, I'll just let them bring it up." This is a crucial mistake. Skeletons hate it when Skins appear to be trying to sweep things under the carpet. When a Skeleton thinks that their Skin is trying to avoid dealing with an issue, the Skin will have a hard time convincing the Skeleton that they really care about the issue when it is brought up. So, Skins, don't ever look like you are avoiding. Bring things up even if it's just an inkling that something is wrong. Be the first one to bring up as many issues as you can. This will move you right into where you want to be—in prevention mode.

Be Releasing, Be Accountable

When it comes to the Skin's schedule, Skeletons should be as releasing as possible. This doesn't mean enabling the Skin to participate in compromising situations. As long as the activities they participate in are not immoral or potentially immoral, give them freedom to live on cruise control, to be independent. Schedule that freedom. Yes, schedule the time for them to be independent and unaccountable. When unaccountability time is scheduled, then it is actually within the framework of accountability, isn't it? So, set them free. Give them space and time just to be themselves.

And Skins, be accountable. Keep your every word and commitment, because that Skeleton of yours is logged into the old mental computer. Ask before you act. Ask before you spend money. Get your Skeleton to buy into your schedule.

These are all areas where weekly staff meetings come in handy. Coordinate your weekly plans with your weekly schedule. Listen to the checks of the Holy Spirit as you communicate with your Skeleton. Don't be so sure of yourself about what you know. If you get a check about something that you were sure about, accept the check. The habit of asking permission is better than the habit of asking for forgiveness.

For both sides, accountability is the way to freedom. Skeletons, be releasing. Skins, be accountable.

Help Wanted! Fruits and Gifts

Sanctified daily by the Holy Spirit, a husband and wife experience dynamic growth both as a couple and individually. As individuals, Skins and Skeletons manifest their growth in uniquely different ways: Skins demonstrate the fruit of the Spirit, while Skeletons excel in the intuitive gifts of the Spirit. Valencia, for example, is so much better than me at creating a loving, peaceful, and patient environment. As a teacher, she is loved by her students because she puts them at ease. They are full of peace because they know that she loves them. While I manufacture intensity and enthusiasm, she creates an environment where the fruit of the Spirit reigns. There's a big difference.

I tend to be concerned about preventing future problems, intuitively sensing when someone is angry or hurt. I am also better than her at creating a sense of order and convenience. This is good, but, while I am creating these good things, I may be making everyone miserable. So, trust me, we need both the Skin and the Skeleton in the home, at work, on the job, even at parties. At a party, you need a bunch of Skins to create fruit, but you also need Skeletons to create intensity and focus. This will prevent the fruit punch from ending up on the carpet.

Loose Cannons?

Skeletons, if they are growers, have a knack for intuition and discernment. They sense, they read, they discern spirits. They see into the future and go into prevention mode whenever and wherever possible. But watch out. As a gift, discernment can bring maximum benefits, but it can also bring everything crashing to earth. How does this happen? Well, if they are not careful, Skeletons will hurt everyone by worrying, stressing out, and constantly reading into everything.

Yes, a Skeleton out of control is a major problem for everyone. And yet, a Skeleton in control can be a modern-day Solomon, full of wisdom and sensitivity. But being that takes some humility and what I call "Skin grafting" — adding Skin-like characteristics to one's Skeletal nature (more on this below).

Live and Let Live

For Skins, having everything in a state of perfect order is simply not the big deal that it is for Skeletons. For them, the issue is how much love, joy, and peace saturates the environment. "If everything isn't perfect," they would say, "don't sweat it. We will live and the world will keep on turning." Skins just know that many problems can't be prevented anyway, so why stress out about the future so much?

But this attitude of Skins can end up disturbing the environment just as much as the overly discerning attitude of Skeletons does. Skeletons create conflict almost out of impulse (feeling it is necessary to prevent future conflict). On their side, Skins avoid conflict until the very last moment, preferring to have a "thick Skin" and letting everything roll off their back. However, finally, after things pile up, Skins will either explode or shut down. To avoid this, what the Skin needs is a "bone implant" — adding Skeleton-like characteristics to one's Skin nature. (more on this below)

What To Do?

The key to holiness for both Skins and Skeletons is to develop in the areas that are holding them back and soar with their natural strengths. This is where "skin grafts" and "bone implants" come in.

My marriage is greater than ever because I've had a skin graft, i.e. I've learned to be more like Valencia — upping the value of spiritual fruit in my life. In so doing, I've come to realize that a loving, peaceful environment is every bit as important in the Kingdom of God as timing, prevention, and discernment. And while I have let my wife rub off on me, I have rubbed off on her. Some of my Skeleton nature — discernment, for example — is at work in her spirit in a much greater measure.

Man, have things ever changed! Thanks to a bone implant from me, she even gets stressed out sometimes!

Rubbing off on one another. Well, that's the way it should be. Couples will either mesh (and become more like each other), or reject (become more set in their ways). When the Bible speaks of bones and flesh, it says that the two should become one. Skeletons, this means you need to grow some fruit, and, Skins, you need to work on discernment.

Become a Superhero!!!

I Have to be Me ...

Here is a question I am asked frequently: *Pastor, are you saying that I should be someone different than I am? Aren't I supposed to be myself?*

This is a valid question. I am definitely *not* saying that you should abandon your God-given personality traits or your gifting. But I am recommending that you patch, repair, and reconfigure your weaknesses. I am advising that you love the other person by being willing to grow and change for their sake.

Love means being willing to adjust a few things in one's self in order to meet the needs of the other person. When you *give* love to your spouse, you will *receive* it back. But if your attitude is, "I'm not going to change for anyone," then your spouse probably won't change anything for you.

Love Don't Come Naturally

Fasten your seatbelt, dear reader. I am about to take you for a ride through the most exciting, innovative, perhaps "edgy" thing that you are going find in this book. Everything else leads to this point. It is simple but profound, and may sound too good to be true. But, in short, it is a *concept of love* that has helped me to be me, and yet enabled me to love my wife.

The concept begins with this premise: basically, we all

want to be married to ourselves. If our spouse were us they would just know, automatically, how to make us feel loved. Unfortunately, because we marry our opposite, according to God's plan, loving each other just doesn't come naturally.

When I came to recognize this, I realized that loving my wife would require radical, drastic action on my part. Somehow, I would have to reach outside of myself to love my wife in the way that she feels loved. Nothing short of that would do.

To be perfectly honest, doing that seemed to me like superhuman effort and I wondered if I were capable of it. But I knew Valencia was worth everything I could give, so I set a new course for my life, my marriage. Superhuman effort would require that I become, in my own way, a superhero.

I Become Spiderman

Superhero? Me? Don't make me laugh! I hear what you are saying. Let me explain how this works. We will use Spiderman as an example.

Spiderman is mostly Peter Parker. When needed, when the pressure is on at different times, Peter pulls off his suit and becomes Spiderman. Now, who is Spiderman? He is Peter Parker. He never stops being Peter Parker. But, *for the sake of loving others*, he shifts into the person that others need him to be.

The same is true in our love relationship. My wife needs me to shift out of being me from time to time and *be her*. She needs me to love her the way in which she feels love. This requires me to be, for a period of time, something that I'm not. I have to put on my Valencia suit and, for as long it takes, act like her, think like her, and feel like her.

By doing this you will become a superhero in the eyes of your spouse! Your spouse will notice that you are crucifying your flesh just for them, and you will gain more respect and love than you can imagine. Believe me, this has happened in my life. My respect, love, and appreciation for my wife are off the charts. And because we have both become super-heroes, she feels the same about me. When needed, we have learned to become the other person for small periods of time in order to make the other feel loved.

The cool thing about this concept of love is that you don't become schizophrenic. Gradually, you begin to put on the qualities that you need. Gradually, you mesh with your su-perhero character, becoming a more holy and mature per-son. Instead of resenting the qualities of your spouse, you start embracing them. In doing so, you become a more Christ-like person.

Marriage is God's great plan for your sanctification, but you have to work the system so the Holy Spirit can work on you. May God bless you as you move into the wonderful arena of a level-four marriage. It is the place we all desire, the level where marriages are literally made and lived in heaven. If you get discouraged, don't allow yourself to stay that way. Remain committed to one another and to the task at hand. Keep on believing, and you will move mountains in your marriage

KEN PETERS is senior pastor of Covenant Church in Spokane, Washington, an affiliate church of Covenant Church in Carrollton, TX. During his 9 years of senior pastoring, God has gifted Ken with a special anointing for marriage and children. He and his wife have been married for over thirteen years and have two children.

Printed in the United States
92120LV00002B/61-75/A